Annmarie Revisions

poems

Greg Watson

Annmarie Revisions

Second Edition

Originally published in 2000 as a chapbook
by
Lockout Press

Credits
Cover Photos: Pixabay
Author Photo: Jordana Torgeson
Layout: Vida Raine

ISBN13: **9798695018462**

Acknowledgements

"Away" previously appeared in
Rock Falls Review

"Arizona," "The Loft," "After Meeting with an Old Love," and "Still Life" appeared in
Sulphur River Literary Review

"Irises" previously appeared in
Spout

"Hands" previously appeared in
Curmudgeon

"Snapshot: Summer, 1974" previously appeared in
Intrepid

"This is Where our Bodies End" previously appeared in
Muse of Fire

"Windows" previously appeared in
Slightly West

"Waking in Hotels" previously appeared in
First Class

"The Morning Has its Own Reasons for Waking" previously appeared in
Free for All

Titles by Greg Watson

All the World at Once: New and Selected Poems

What Music Remains

The Distance Between Two Hands

Things You Will Never See Again

Pale Light from a Distant Room

Cold Water Memory

Annmarie Revisions

Open Door, Open Wall

Many titles available from Amazon and Nodin Press

www.amazon.com

www.NodinPress.com

Other Contributions

The Road by Heart: Poems of Fatherhood

Edited by Greg Watson and Richard Broderick

published by Nodin Press

CONTENTS

A CLASSIC QUESTION

"Ingenium Nobis ipsa puella facit."
Propertius wrote that it's the girl who makes the
poems. But is the obverse true? Will poems make
a girl? I'm really not so certain about that.

-James Laughlin

ONCE

In that year the sun was a lion
yawning at our feet;
the moon was bruised
and the waters swam with sudden light.
A quiet woman of old world sorrow
played an out of tune violin
every morning as we dressed.
No books were written, no records kept.
What we needed, we invented;
what we could not use was sealed for museums.
Every act was doomed to be repeated
until mistakes were perfected.

In that year everything was younger
and blissfully unaware.
You were lipstick sweating gin,
I a flickering shadow in search of a form.
We fell in love simply to feel
more alive, and parted like two who
had seen the same ghost.

AWAY

The shirt you once wore will
always smell like you,
of saltwater, musk, and candle wax,
the print of your dress
fluttering with a thousand moths
racing toward the light.
Every word we spoke lingers
like sunshine and smoke,
neither rising nor falling away.
The walls are blank
canvases once again,
clear and open as the sky.
But I never wanted to write
the story of us, never bargained
with logic or continuity,
nor with an ending
that would seem in any way
believable.

APRICOT

When I think of your long, elegant
fingers combing through
your sun-tangled hair, I want
to stay within that light forever,
the sky open for miles,
the birds like shifting absences
along the green horizon,
and the sweet taste of apricot
held close against my lips.

ARIZONA

We drove all day with the sun at our backs,
hours passing like a slow-moving dream,
past red clay madonnas and the sandy feet of God,
on through the poverty and wonder
of Navajo land, through the backdrop
of John Ford's mythical America.
At the trading post outside of Flagstaff
they sold wooden crucifixes
beside half-melted Hershey bars
and belt buckles made from hood ornaments.
I bought ghost beads and went shirtless,
crawled atop a mound of stone
and parted the clouds with my hands.
"Beginner's luck," you laughed.
We brought whiskey and beer into the rez,
not knowing better, and watched
the sun set like a cosmological cocktail.
Later, we slept in your mother's adobe,
cats jumping in and out of the washing machine
as a light blue snow fell upon the mountains,
and we slept the strangely settled sleep
of strangers -- not to each other
but to the rest of the world left behind,
the exact cross-stitch where
the long-stretched skin of the desert ends,
pushed ever backward by heavy-shouldered
buildings, great rivers named for men,
asthmatic cities with gravestone sidewalks,
and the endless highways required
to somehow keep them from falling apart.

GLINT

The smallest things come now
to make themselves known:
a slash of light falling
across your sleeveless black dress
the evening that we met,
its fabric textured like a map
that goes on and on
until all maps are burned.
The smallest things grow
large among such absence.
Now, I clean the razors
from the cold of the bathroom,
the mysterious potions left behind,
scraps of tissue smudged
in charcoal, faded rouge.
No one tells you that this is how
it ends, the solemn work of
removal, of cleansing surfaces,
opening the windows
to let our voices walk free.
Would we have listened?
I suspect that we would have
continued driving headlong,
simply to feel the lines of the world
begin to blur, the wind
shooting through us, erasing
our names again and again.

UNDER THE SKIN

Like the unseen shards
of glass broken
weeks ago, I still get
sharp reminders
of you, of me.
Nothing is ever gone;
nothing is ever
swept clean.

THIS IS WHERE OUR BODIES END

We lie together like hands too weary
to applaud, hinged but
uncertain now of our purpose.
We know this is the last time, though
we do not speak it.
Already I feel that I am dreaming
of you, dreaming so much
more intimate than the physical,
this body that for moments
outside of time I love more than trees
or sky, the constant shift of
seasons upon the skin,
the endless turning
impossible to keep up with.
Only this time our bodies follow:
the spooky burnt earth tones
of autumn, or winter
in its white and stately ticktock.
Yet I am tangled in this moment between,
the silver armor of bracelets and rings,
the sweet-salty smell of your hair,
the thoughtless sighs overtaking
our speech, an unspoken reminder
of beauty and luxury
we must now give up, of all
that is already lost.

THE ROOMS

Before faces, before form, we
remember the rooms,
modest and unassuming
but offering their simple comfort
to all who passed through.
Once, that included you and me,
sharing our breath between
walls cool to the touch,
no matter the season,
sharing the shabby green sofa
and beaten-down chair,
more springs than thread,
you used to laugh.
Could it be that what falls away
is best remembered,
becoming what it always was:
warm sunlit shelves filled
with poetry and obscure saints
neither of us could name,
your charcoal sketches scattered
everywhere, the smoke
and floral scent of your body
foreign to me, then as now.
These are the rooms in which you
loved me, and then didn't; these
are the places I return to and don't.
I can almost see the man I was
on the peripheral of thought,
painfully young and expectant,
walking those narrow steps
for the first time, waiting, waiting.
How I envy his not knowing.

BETWEEN TIMES

At times our lives are in unison,
the rhythm of our speech right in time,
body to body, breath to breath.
Lying fallow in wanton love
I accept, I take it all in,
the purest antidote for caustic grief,
the hedonist's fervor that shakes
the black years to ash.
Yet on gray days there is distance,
there is silence between spaces no wider
than flesh. We bruise more easily,
wear our clothing like battle flags,
our jewelry like armor;
the scar on my arm raised
like a stem beneath the skin,
the bruise upon your thigh
a glinting shard of moonlight
wrapped in rainbow wax.
Though faith returns, begging and joyful,
the seemingly random way sunlight
hits a warehouse in Lowertown,
or the ocean, how it reaches its furthest
destination without thinking, yielding only
to itself, continually beginning.
Fire for fire, measure for measure,
I would not change it;
I would not trade it.
Not for silver, not for gold,
not for any world that I know.

HANDS

The hands, you tell me, the hands
are glass keys, the navigators of distance,
weather vanes of wind, rain, and secret heart,
the framework of knotted fists.
The hands say more than eyes, movement,
or sexual longing combined.
You are right, I reluctantly agree;
but the hands linger too long for safety.
They grope, grab, grapple with memories
that the mind cannot recall,
reaching for all they do not need,
in search of warmth between the flesh
of good womanly thighs
in the uncertain breath before dawn,
the same hours that drove ancient men
to madness — on wayward ships,
and the cold echo of limestone cells.
Sever them, good woman;
they are too raw, too fleeting.
They are too much responsibility.

NAME

I do not wish to be
redundant, I just like
to say your name,
to feel the warmth
of it resonating
in my throat;
and on quiet nights
when the world
forgets itself,
I speak its many
variations at once.

WAKING IN HOTELS

It's strange, waking in a room not your own
in a city likewise not your own,
distant even to itself; forgetting for a moment
where you are or even your name,
a lonesome cricket playing its single note
above the air conditioner's hum.
The rooms are always deceptively clean,
the bath tubs too small, the ceilings
too low, so that even your dreams remain
grounded, circling until daylight.
It's strange in New Orleans, where
the distant strains of brass bands
can be heard until morning;
it's strange in San Francisco, where
the sun struggles blindly through the fog,
and skinny, smoking men hammer at
the heads of stinking fish
before you can open your eyes.
It's strange in your own hometown
when there's nowhere else to go,
celebrating or mourning
something you no longer recall,
looking out across the billowing smoke
of red brick factories and homes,
across the same gray streets
you've walked since you were able,
never quite getting used to them.
It's strange and it's sad and it's glorious,
how memory begins long before
anyone leaves, the way
some leaving takes a lifetime;
and when I can no longer see your face

in my mind's eye is when I need
you the most, and there's nothing left
to do but write it all down,
pray for rest, let the room hold
with whatever warmth it can offer.

WINDOWS

Now that you are gone, everything
in the apartment echoes,
as if there were a second body
here after all, sound following sound,
motion imitating motion.
The windows are stripped clean,
open to the gray-blue world
outside, the wind lifting the leaves
and the clothes on the line
as it always has.

Do you remember our first night here,
how you were certain that these
rooms were haunted?
You sat upright in bed half the night,
startled by every ping and pop,
walls shifting in and out of sleep,
the clang and gurgle of ancient radiators
struggling to keep us warm?

Only now do I realize that maybe
you were right, hearing
what you once heard, weighted with
the presence of absence.
I light the candles, as you once did,
put blue glass along the windows,
transcribing all that the wind
may have to say.

SNAPSHOT: SUMMER, 1974

This was always your favorite photograph,
the one you carried with you
when you needed to be reminded
of that place within yourself,
a calm and sacred space
in constant need of reclamation.
Here you are a child of five, maybe six,
your face a squinting smile lit with summer,
your body small and thin,
arms cradling your beloved cat,
shapeless and smoke-colored
against the bird bone of your chest.
Sunlight pours through your ears,
your collarbone a small wave of shadow,
your bare feet held calmly to the earth.
There is no fear, no terror.
That would come later, and would
not be spoken of for decades.
In this moment, all that matters
is the endless expanse of daylight,
the green fields surrounding
you on all sides, begging to be explored,
land so flat that you could run
and run for miles, and never
quite be out of sight.

AFTER MEETING WITH AN OLD LOVE

What to say now of the years stretched
between us — the ladder of slowly dimming
light, years spent in separate cities
and time zones, inventing our stories
among the flesh of others?
Shall we number them, categorize,
give proper names, as though
they were ages within themselves?
We of course have aged, in small but
certain ways — the thin lines intersecting
across outstretched hands, the borders
around eyes softened by work and worry;
those who we once were seemingly
written off in time's endless revisions.
We do not speak of such things,
our words remaining pleasant but slight
in this musty cafe, sipping chamomile tea
as the city outside swells with snow,
like dim, white ashes falling from the pages
of an endless book, and the memory
of the love between us is every
word that we failed to read.

THE LOFT

The winters were the worst, outwardly bitter,
jealous, minimalist to a fault
as we waded through, cold-damp clinging,
speaking softly as hostages,
staying in bed for hours unending.
We were not ill but in love,
a separate and higher calling of illness
(or so I imagined in the fervor
of youth). The landmarks of your body
I knew and knew again — memorizing
what I could, yet could never fully know.
If I dressed or read books or bothered with food,
I was a fool. I should have known all along
the dangers inherent, that the slightest
of movements could startle you awake.
Though it was, while it was, bliss:
black veils and roses hung upon the walls
like crosses, there in that simple room,
cathedral-high ceilings and Bach's death mask
gazing eyelessly toward the door,
toward the sprawling, snowbound city,
silent and deaf in its death-like knowledge,
as if all I say now were somehow foreseeable.

ROUGE

You say that the past
is the past, but that
is not really true.
Tonight I drank whiskey
for the first time
in years, and tasted
your lipstick on
the rim of the glass.

DAMAGE

The only part of me
left standing
was the part that I had
long neglected;
the only part left
unbroken
was the part that
no hand could touch,
whether by love
or by harm, one who
would not answer
to my name
in a million years.

THE PERFUME OF LONELINESS

I have discovered that absence
too has a fragrance which lingers,
even in the smallest places.
It is the residue of everything
now departed, the brush-fire memory
of a woman's face and hands,
scent of rosewater and swamp-musk,
the secret sweetness of earth
shifting its body into night,
and unlike the long migrations
of dream, refuses to lie down,
refuses to sleep on anything but air.

GHOST STORY

Our love is a ghost
story now;
but I still like
telling it every now
and then.

CROWDS

When exactly did all women become one
and one woman become all? It is
as if each body were threaded together
by strands of invisible light,
the way crowds sometimes blur
in the shimmering heat of late summer —
each memory a shard that reflects the other.
I love you now with the love
of thousands, and speak your name
even in the names of others.

ASCENSION

I've been asleep all winter, an unnamed
sorrow bleached as elephant bone,
brittle as the crunch of glass
beneath a frozen work boot.
Frost has grown inside the windows.
Every night in my dreams I have constructed
cathedrals in which to bury my dead,
I have shoveled hot coals
until my hands bled
black ribbons of daylight.

Now, even the cat looks holy,
an enlightened silvery cloud following
the light across the floor.
I open every window, as if to quench
a thirst; the uncertain air
strangely foreign to my senses —
stale smoke and copper, musty roses,
old money. Papers scatter,
buds sprout from the spines
of long-abandoned books.
Even the sun squints to see me better.

BLAZE

When love burns
the whole house down,
you don't go
back in looking
for trinkets.

IRISES

The irises that you sent sit beside
the typewriter, vibrant yet
somehow solemn, weeping silently among
themselves, their thin purple skins
heavy with sunlight.
It's true that I've been ill,
the world within and without
suddenly upon me,
its reckless weather tumbling through
the plainsongs of the mind.
I have stayed in bed for hours
with this old, blue notebook,
crawled into the self and called it home.
I turned the sun down to low
and drank from the cool, gray stars.
But I accept the challenge
of these flowers, wild and stubborn,
rustling as if a moth, a tiger,
a mad laugh were to leap
suddenly to life.

THE MORNING HAS ITS OWN REASONS FOR WAKING

One by one, the shadows arrive
with the light, filling the room in odd angles,
hastily drawn corners, as if the sun
had risen on a sinking ship.
We lie blanketed in early summer,
our bodies languid and humid
beneath damp cotton sheets,
the air saturated with the smell
of longing, and its resolution.
The earth is shifting almost audibly;
and all along the freeway cars melt into
each other like silver constellations,
outlines of inverted stars
disappearing in puffs of smoke.
There is the faintest of sorrows descending,
small enough to fit within a sigh,
a turning of the body while somehow
looking in neither direction.
But I am content that there are no
decisions to be made today,
no words flashing their dull blades.
The cats need to be fed;
the daylight waits to be entered.

STILL LIFE

A good rain gives the impression that
something is at last happening,
or at least about to happen.
Though tonight the rain has little to say
as I sit here in this old red chair,
at this shipwrecked desk,
one bare bulb dangling above my head.
I am calming down, winding down,
talking to myself in a low monotone.

There hasn't always been time to think.
Often there has been the threat
of poverty, unemployment,
of the last remnants of a strained romance.
For many years self-destruction clung
like a bad shadow. Now older,
I contemplate the size and measure of my days
and have little to say.
The fear of aging diminishes with age,
and suicide is for the young.
But tonight the rain drones on,
the night leans heavily into the room
and it feels like life. And nothing happens.

Greg Watson is the author of eight collections of poetry, most recently *All the World at Once: New and Selected Poems.* He is also co-editor with Richard Broderick of *The Road by Heart: Poems of Fatherhood*, published by Nodin Press.

Connect with Greg

Instagram
@gregwatsonpoet

Other Titles
available at

www.amazon.com
and
www.NodinPress.com

www.ingramcontent.com/pod-product-compliance
Lightning Source LLC
LaVergne TN
LVHW020533160826
845677LV00015B/4042

* 9 7 9 8 6 9 5 0 1 8 4 6 2 *